Miss Colfax's Light

AIMÉE BISSONETTE AND *Illustrated by* EILEEN RYAN EWEN

PUBLISHED *by* SLEEPING BEAR PRESS

Sleeping Bear Press™

2395 South Huron Parkway, Suite 200, Ann Arbor, MI 48104
www.sleepingbearpress.com
© Sleeping Bear Press

Printed and bound in the United States.
10 9 8 7 6 5 4 3 2 1

Library of Congress Cataloging-in-Publication Data

Names: Bissonette, Aimée M., author. | Ewen, Eileen Ryan, illustrator.
Title: Miss Colfax's light / written by Aimée Bissonette ; illustrated by Eileen Ryan Ewen.
Description: Ann Arbor, MI : Sleeping Bear Press, [2016] | Audience: Ages 6-10.-
Identifiers: LCCN 2015027640 | ISBN 9781585369553
Subjects: LCSH: Colfax, Harriet, 1824-1905—Juvenile literature. | Michigan
City Lighthouse (Michigan City, Ind.)—Juvenile literature. | Women
lighthouse keepers—Indiana—Michigan City—Biography—Juvenile
literature. | Lighthouses—Indiana—Michigan City—History—Juvenile
literature. | Michigan City (Ind.)—Biography—Juvenile literature.
Classification: LCC VK1025.M47 B57 2016 | DDC 386/.8550977291—dc23
LC record available at http://lccn.loc.gov/2015027640

For Bryan, who loves lighthouses.

Special thanks to Jim, Karen, Vera, Jacqueline, and the Michigan City Historical Society.

—Aimée

For my mother, Jeanne C. Ryan, the strongest woman I know. Thank you for always reminding me, "I can do this."

— Eileen

Harriet Colfax stood before the Michigan City Lighthouse, bag in hand. The wind blew in off the lake. It wrapped her long skirt and petticoats around her legs.

The cream-colored lighthouse was three years old. Bricklayers had built the construction date, 1858, right into the wall. Harriet had watched them build the lighthouse. Now, here she stood a few years later with all of her belongings.

Harriet was 37 years old. She had no job and no place to live. She had come to the Indiana frontier with her brother and worked with him at his newspaper. When her brother got sick, he shut down the newspaper and moved away. But Harriet loved Indiana. She couldn't leave!

If Harriet left Indiana, she'd lose all the independence she'd gained. She'd be without her friend, a schoolteacher named Ann Hartwell. And she'd be much too far from the crystal-blue beauty of Lake Michigan.

If Harriet stayed in Indiana, she could make a life. Here in Indiana women could do nearly anything men could. Here she had been a music teacher and newspaper worker. And now she could be a lighthouse keeper. She could put a roof over her own head — and Ann's — and earn $350 a year if she was willing to work for it. Harriet was willing to work for it.

Harriet drew in a long breath, closed her eyes, and exhaled slowly.

"I can do this," she said, walking up to the front door.

Harriet wasted no time learning her lighthouse duties. The lives of ship captains and sailors depended on her. And Michigan City depended on those ships. She knew there were some in town who doubted her. She was small and delicate looking. She had no experience. And many thought she got the job only because her cousin was a U.S. Congressman. Harriet would prove them wrong.

Twice each night,
Harriet carried whale oil
in a bucket up narrow stairs
to the top of the lantern tower.
There she polished the Fresnel lens
and refueled the light.

At daybreak, she climbed back up the stairs and put the light out. Then she cleaned and painted.

She varnished the woodwork and shined the brass.
She made notes in her log.

When evening rolled around, she started all over again.

Night after night, Harriet climbed the narrow stairs. She climbed when she was tired. She climbed when she was ill. She climbed when waves battered the beach, the wind rattled the windows, and cold seeped in under the door of the tiny house. Each night the light had to be lit. Harriet's hands grew calloused and her legs grew strong.

"I can do this," she said.

Over the years, Harriet's lighthouse duties grew. In November of 1871, a beacon light was installed on the Michigan City east pier. Now Harriet was responsible for that light, too. A "catwalk" was built of wood and mounted high on metal struts atop the pier. It ran the length of the pier—1,500 feet out into the lake. The beacon light was at the end of the catwalk.

October 13, 1872:
Northerly gale, continuing all day and all night. Weather cold with rain and hail storms. Gale perfectly fearful by nightfall—waves dashed over the top of the beacon—reached the beacon in imminent risk tonight as the waves ran over the elevated walk.

August 16, 1873:
A strong wind & high sea.
Became drenched by the
waves in going down to Light
the Beacon.

Now each night, after lighting the main light, Harriet filled another bucket with fuel for the beacon light. Lard oil had replaced whale oil by then. It was cheaper and easier to get. But lard oil had to be heated. In the worst weather, the wind howled and waves crashed over the catwalk, soaking Harriet's clothes. Sometimes the lard oil hardened in the cold and Harriet had to fight back through the wind to reheat the oil.

In 1874 the Lighthouse Board ordered another change. The beacon light was moved to Michigan City's west pier. The west pier was on the far side of Trail Creek. It extended 500 more feet into Lake Michigan. Now each night, after lighting the main light, Harriet had to row a small boat across the creek, hike the far shore, and cross a longer catwalk to light the beacon light.

December 5, 1885:
Gale continues, with snow—cold. Elevated walk badly damaged & beacon & light put out. The beacon cannot be repaired this fall. Telegraphed the Inspector.

March 21, 1886:
Str. Westerly gale, snow squalls & blizzard—cold. 150' superstructure of W. pier carried away by the storm.

Sometimes storms damaged the catwalk
and area piers, scattering debris across the lake.

Sometimes the Lighthouse Inspector allowed Harriet to hire an assistant to help with the beacon light. But many times he said "no," leaving the difficult work of tending both lights to Harriet alone. Work had become scarce for men on the frontier. Was the Lighthouse Board trying to make Harriet quit so they could give her job to a man? Harriet didn't quit.

"I can do this," she said.

One stormy night in 1886, when Harriet was more than 60 years old, she set out for the west pier. The wind raged. Driving sleet covered her coat with ice. Sand from the dunes along the lake pelted Harriet's face, stinging her cheeks. She struggled with her lantern and bucket. Her boots slipped and slid on the catwalk.

The beacon tower swayed in the wind as Harriet struck her match and lit the light. Teeth chattering from the cold, she hurried back across the catwalk. When she stepped off the catwalk, a deafening screech filled the air.

Crash!

Harriet spun around. The beacon tower had ripped from its moorings and crashed into the lake.

All that night Harriet paced the lighthouse floors. She climbed to the top of the lantern tower over and over to check the main light. Anyone out on the lake in this storm would need her light to guide them. Harriet would not let them down.

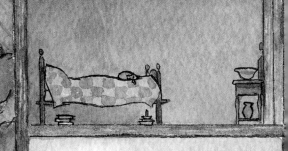

October 14, 1886:
Severe Southeast wind and rain storm this morning and severe westerly gale this afternoon. The beacon structure was carried away in the storm and thrown up on the beach, a <u>wreck</u>. The temporary light also carried away.

For 43 years Harriet kept the Michigan City light burning. The people of Michigan City came to call the lighthouse "Miss Colfax's Light." Ship captains called it "Old Faithful."

With Ann as her companion, Harriet lived out her life on the great lake. Through the years she saw storms and destruction, but also brilliant sunsets, lunar eclipses, and silent, dancing northern lights. She saw tall-masted schooners with white sails give way to steamships of iron and steel.

In 1904, when Harriet was 80 years old, the Lighthouse Board put one more change into place. The Michigan City Lighthouse would be replaced by a modern light. The new light would have a steam engine and boilers and a fog whistle. It would have huge coal-fired furnaces. It would require the work of several keepers.

Harriet's era had ended. "Miss Colfax's Light" was to be no more.

POST O

June 27, 1904:
Work on the foundation for fog signal structure commenced.

August 6, 1904:
Dwelling house becoming almost uninhabitable from repairing going on.

Standing in the lighthouse kitchen, the tiny lighthouse keeper fought back her tears. Her back was bowed from years of stoking fires, climbing stairs and catwalks, and carrying buckets in the cold.

She had spent almost every night for the past 43 years awake and watching, protecting the sailors and ships out on the lake. How would she ever learn to close her eyes and rest at the end of the day?

But Harriet understood. She was 80 years old. It was time.

October 1, 1904:
Tendered my resignation of
the main light to the Lt. House
Inspector, the same to take effect
October 13, 1904.

October 8, 1904:
Sold household effects preparatory
to vacating the dear old Lt. House.

Harriet packed her bags and checked the last tasks off her list. She took a final glance around the room. Then she drew in her breath, closed her eyes, and exhaled slowly.

"I can do this," she said.

Harriet placed the keys to the lighthouse on the table and walked out the door.

Author's Note

Harriet Colfax was not a typical lighthouse keeper. There have been many women lighthouse keepers in our nation's history. Most of them became keepers because their husbands or fathers were keepers. But Harriet was appointed. Her cousin, Schuyler Colfax, was a U.S. Congressman who later became Vice President. He probably helped Harriet get her job as a favor to Harriet's family.

Harriet was also better educated than most keepers. Her log is famous for the detail it provides. She describes the shooting of President Garfield in July of 1881 and "draping the lighthouse in mourning" when he and other presidents died. Her log entry from July 4, 1896, tells how she "floated to the breeze" for the first time the "new" U.S. flag with 45 stars.

But Harriet was like other keepers in the work she did. Lighthouse keeping was difficult, dangerous work. It is remarkable she worked every day, around the clock, for more than forty years tending her light. In October 1904, a *Chicago Tribune* reporter asked Harriet about her life as a lighthouse keeper. Harriet said, "I love the lamps, the old lighthouse, and the work. They are the habit, the home, everything dear I have known for so long. . . . I would rather die here than live elsewhere."

Harriet died on April 16, 1905, only six short months after she retired as Michigan City Lighthouse keeper and less than three months after the death of her dear friend, Ann. Harriet and Ann are buried near one another in Michigan City's Greenwood Cemetery and the lighthouse is now a museum where visitors can learn more about Harriet and her life in the 1800s. In all her years of service, Harriet's Michigan City light never failed to shine.

Glossary of Lighthouse Terms

Beacon light: A light placed on land, a pier, or a buoy to warn ships of dangerous areas and guide them into harbors.

Breakwater: A man-made structure of stone or concrete built off-shore. It shelters a shore area or harbor by breaking the force of incoming waves.

Catwalk: A narrow walkway that is often raised high above the ground.

Fog whistle: A signal that uses sound to warn ships away from rocks and other dangerous areas when it is foggy.

Fresnel lens: A circular glass lens that looks like a giant beehive with a lamp inside. It was invented in 1822 by Augustin-Jean Fresnel of France.

Lantern tower: A room surrounded by windows that houses the lighthouse lamp and lens.

Lighthouse Board: A nine-member board created by Congress in 1852, it appointed lighthouse keepers, and hired inspectors and engineers.

Log (a journal): A kind of diary used by lighthouse keepers for daily notes. Logs were used to track inspections, ship traffic, visitors, the weather, and other events.

Pier: A structure built out into the water that is used as a docking place for boats or to protect or form a harbor.